Sharks

by Rose Lewis

Contents

Pioneer Valley Educational Press, Inc.

WHAT IS A SHARK?

A shark is a kind of fish.
Sharks can be found in every ocean
and in some rivers and lakes.
Most fish have bones, but sharks do not.
Sharks have **cartilage** instead of bones.
Cartilage is not as hard as bones.

SHARK ANATOMY

There are many kinds of sharks.
Some sharks are as small as a person's hand.
Some sharks are bigger than a bus.
Sharks' bodies can be many different shapes.

Most sharks have torpedo-shaped bodies
that glide easily through the water.
Some sharks have flattened bodies
that allow them to hide in the sand
on the ocean floor.

Here are the body parts of a typical shark.

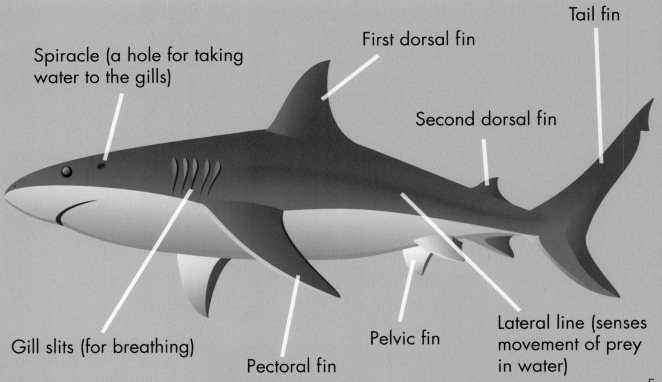

Spiracle (a hole for taking water to the gills)

First dorsal fin

Tail fin

Second dorsal fin

Gill slits (for breathing)

Pectoral fin

Pelvic fin

Lateral line (senses movement of prey in water)

5

THE SENSES OF A SHARK

Sharks have many senses. Like humans, they can see, hear, smell, taste, and touch. But sharks also have senses humans do not have. A shark's senses make it one of the best hunters in the world.

Sharks can hear **low-frequency** sounds and can smell even a tiny bit of blood in the water. Sharks can also sense **vibrations** in the ocean water. These senses help the shark to find its prey.

It can be difficult to see deep in the ocean, where it is dark. Sharks have special eyes to see better in dim light.

Sharks also have a sense called electroreception. All living animals give off small electrical signals. Sharks can sense another animal's electrical signals. Sharks use this sense to find hiding **prey**.

SHARK TEETH

Sharks have up to 3,000 teeth.
They never run out of teeth. If a tooth comes out,
another comes forward from a back row of teeth.
Most sharks do not chew their food.
They swallow their food whole.

SHARK ATTACK

Many people are afraid of being attacked by a shark, but shark attacks are not very common.

The most dangerous sharks are
the great white shark, the tiger shark,
the bull shark, and the oceanic whitetip shark.

The bull shark is the shark that most often attacks people. Sometimes bull sharks swim in shallow water where people swim.

Why do you think sharks sometimes attack people? Sharks might be thinking people on surfboards are seals or sea lions, some of their favorite food.
When a shark attacks, it arches its back and throws back its head.
This places its mouth in a better position for taking a bite.

Tiger Shark

HABITAT

Some sharks live deep in the water. Some live on, or near, the ocean floor, and some live near the ocean surface.

Some sharks will swim many miles into freshwater rivers.

Blacktip Reef Shark

Some sharks live in warm water,
while others live in cool water.
Some sharks stay in the same area
all of their lives, while others travel across oceans.

13

SHARK BABIES

Baby sharks are called pups. They are born in three different ways.

Some shark pups grow inside the mother shark, just like a human baby.

Some shark pups start out as eggs and are laid to hatch, like a baby bird.

Some pups start as eggs that hatch inside their mother and then are born.

Sharks do not take care of their babies after they are born, but they do search for a safe place to lay their eggs or to give birth.

Glossary

cartilage: a firm but flexible tissue found in many animals

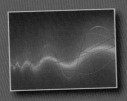

low frequency: a small number of vibrations each second

prey: an animal hunted for food

vibration: to move rhythmically and steadily to and fro